T.C

& other poems

Poetry books by the author

Gullible Skeptic (2001)
Captain Fascist and the Plastic Storm Troopers (2002)
The Cosmopolitan Day of Reckoning (2003)
Mr. Rubik's House of Cards (2004)
Like Darwin Among the Gods (2005)
The Language of Sparrows (2006)
T.O. Loveless & Other Poems (2007)

# T.O. Loveless
## & other poems

### Andreas Gripp

harmonia press

*T.O. Loveless & other poems*
© 2007 by Andreas Michael Gripp

All Rights Reserved. No part of this publication may be reproduced in any form, with the exception of excerpts for the purpose of literary review, without the expressed permission of the publisher.

Published by Harmonia Press, London, Ontario
email: harmonia@execulink.com

author website: www.andreasgripp.com

Title & Back Page Sketches: Tomoko Yonezawa
Cover Photographer: unknown

First Printing, February 2007

Printed in Canada by Double Q Printing
and Graphics, London, Ontario

Library and Archives Canada Cataloguing in Publication

Gripp, Andreas
        T.O. Loveless & other poems / Andreas Gripp.

ISBN 978-0-9739932-2-6

    I. Title. II. Title: T.O. Loveless and other poems.

PS8563.R5563T6 2007    C811'.54    C2007-900243-9

## *Acknowledgements*

Earlier versions of the following poems have appeared in my first four books:

*Fish Out of Water, At the Tone …, She's the Bookworm of Santo Domingo* and *Franklin Stein* from *Gullible Skeptic*

*A Station Wagon's Dead Transmission, Pacifica, Maybe, Penny & the Englishman, Just Another Coup d'état, Chelsea and Liverpool, Decaf to Go* and *The Artists' Long Weekend* from *Captain Fascist and the Plastic Storm Troopers*

*Just Friends, Unborn Daughter, Queens & Richmond* and *Bitter Jeez Louise* from *The Cosmopolitan Day of Reckoning*

*Seven Day Rental, William of Carlton Press, Trumpet Player* and *One Nine-Hundred* from *Mr. Rubik's House of Cards*

The following poems first appeared in the *Past Life Aggression* chapbook: *Orange Hall 585, Vodka Bill, On Our Meeting in the Lunchtime Rush* and *The Substitute*

These poems have appeared in the following publications:

*Moss* in the *Spirit Valley Rambles* anthology, edited by Katherine L. Gordon

*His and Hers* in *Carousel* (#21, University of Guelph)

| | |
|---|---|
| And then there was light | 1 |
| T.O. Loveless | 2 |
| Duracell and the Energizer Bunny | 4 |
| A Station Wagon's Dead Transmission | 6 |
| The Death of Bears and Poetry | 7 |
| My Cat is Half-Greek,<br>    or Zeus left the Acropolis open again | 8 |
| The excuse I use<br>    to avoid cleaning under the stairs | 10 |
| His and Hers | 12 |
| Fish Out of Water | 13 |
| Just Friends | 14 |
| Maybe | 16 |
| Seven Day Rental | 17 |
| November Rose | 18 |
| Moss | 19 |
| For Mr. Bannister, who delivers flowers<br>    to most of the people on my block | 20 |
| Penny & The Englishman | 21 |
| On the Difference a Single Minute Can Make | 22 |
| For every poet who knows what it's like | 24 |
| William of Carlton Press | 26 |
| Bullets | 28 |
| They Asked Me to Write a Poem Against<br>    the War but I Only Came Up With This | 30 |
| Just another coup d'état | 32 |
| Orange Hall, 585 | 34 |
| Unborn Daughter, or Why I Live with Cats | 36 |

| | |
|---|---|
| Trumpet Player | 37 |
| This is all you learned<br>      from your trip to the tabloid stand | 38 |
| Chelsea and Liverpool | 40 |
| At the Tone: 17 hours, 46 minutes,<br>      Coordinated Universal Time | 41 |
| 12/01/07 | 42 |
| Decaf to Go | 43 |
| Queens & Richmond | 44 |
| The Artists' Long Weekend | 45 |
| Bitter Jeez Louise | 46 |
| The Substitute | 47 |
| She's the Bookworm of Santo Domingo | 48 |
| Alexander Schmidt | 50 |
| On Our Search for Leonard Cohen<br>      and Maybe One of His Many Lovers | 52 |
| Franklin Stein | 54 |
| Vodka Bill | 56 |
| The Violinist | 57 |
| On Our Meeting in the Lunchtime Rush | 58 |
| The Devotion | 60 |
| One Nine-Hundred | 61 |
| Listening | 62 |
| The haiku I just wrote is pointless | 63 |
| Tokyo | 64 |
| Pacifica | 66 |

# Foreword

*T.O. Loveless* is one of numerous "character portraits" I've done in my poetry since my first book appeared six years ago. There are many others as well, some of which I've brought back for a second showing in this latest collection.

Almost half of the poems included herein are previous works I may have revised, some favourites of mine from my first four volumes. Over half, though, are brand new, and with the aforementioned create an overview of living in 2007. As always, there is the socio-political, the snapshot of nature, the irony of time, and the relationship gone awry.

Look for the linings of silver scattered about here … there is a little more hope conveyed than what appears on the surface, not necessarily all of the time, but at times when it's necessary.


Andreas Gripp
February 2007

**And then there was light**

With your hands wrist-deep
in fertile soil,
you tell me your daughter passed away
at dawn, on a day that our star
rose without hindering cloud,
and you mused that morning,
before you sadly went and found her,
stiff as a petrified trunk
and her unblinking eyes
locked upon the ceiling,
that to call it "sun" is a misnomer,
for it's connected to *Mother* Earth,
and either "u" or "o", it says the same
masculine thing.

It's the *female*
that reproduces,
you said, gives seeds a place
to call home.

"Daughter," you decreed,
*call it Daughter.*
It will surely love us more
and our weeping will be greater
on the days it isn't there.

## T.O. Loveless

Milk and honey
may not be what she's seeking,
but the allure of something greater,
the pitch of whispered promise,
the possibility that a caress
or more awaits her
at the bus and subway stops,
gives rise to her Spring arrival.

Four million-plus
in a bubbling soup
of freeways, gangs and guns
makes the roar of traffic
a requiem.

Follow me, for her stride
is easy to trail,
and if you vow a restless silence,
I'll show you her quaint apartment
on the seedy side of Queen.

At dusk,
with her bedroom lamp
crackling
from a socket's poor connection,
you can see her
through the spaces
that horizontal blinds
can give,
when they're plastic and they're bent,
when they're fused
with un-wipe-able dust,
when the cracks emitted
give nosy eyes
a peek at her nakedness.

Let's embrace temptation
and catch her disfigurement:
it's in the way she clasps her flesh
and reaches for men who aren't there;
a deep-set scar that only appears
in *appointed,* halogen lighting,
in a monstrous, high-rise apartment,
or a crumbling, side street walkup
with considerably cheaper rent,

the kind reserved for coffee clerks
who've never had a meaningful kiss,
who've never had a silly song
or rhyming verse
inscribed for them,

whose exodus to Metropolis
is bound to disappoint,
the exhaust from cars
and the groan of their horns
filling a pair of seeking senses;

while mouldy mirrors
satiate sight,
breaking glass
takes the place of touch,

blood, taste.

## Duracell and the Energizer Bunny

The battery
in my kitchen clock
has run out of power,
meaning the hands
are all stuck in time
as if they were lodged
in Cretaceous amber
or entrapped
in Pleistocene ice.

On my kitchen wall,
it reads 2:23 pm.
It will forever be 2:23
if I neglect to change
the 9-volt, if I decide
that 2:23 pm
was a grand moment of existence,
and I wish to preserve it
for posterity,

that somewhere on this Earth,
enemies made their peace
after years
of refusing to speak,
that a kitten was saved
from a smelly cage
at a decrepit animal shelter,

that lovers consummated their union,
conceived a baby yet to be born,
one who'd show the world
how hating and killing
can belong to the *past*
(and the world will actually listen!).

I circle the block
around my home
and think of my state of being,
how it's locked in that magical minute
the very second I walk in my house,
how the planet outside
is at breakneck speed
to yet another violent clash;

how I haven't any use
for copper-top cells
or bobbing, drum-playing rabbits;

that whichever lasts the longest
is the ultimate loser
in the ever-approaching end.

## A Station Wagon's Dead Transmission

The car broke down today,
on a cold, pre-Winter morning,
and left us with options three:

We catch a bus and learn the ropes
of never-ever staring,
of leaning left and right
when staggering turns
are made at red,
of pretending not to notice
when the man beside us slobbers
as he speaks,
to neither you or I
or anyone in-between.

We take our bikes out from the shed
and put our lives at stake,
looking out for racing trucks
and jeeps that honk
their harried horns,
that run us off the road
and to an icy curbside tumble,
wrought with bumps and cuts
and shaken nerves.

Third and final pains us most:
we walk in awkward silence,
the crunch of frosted sod,
the small-talk that we mutter
*saying* we are strangers,
each step along the path
revealing all that's lost
and wanting.

## The Death of Bears and Poetry

The teddy bear in my closet
can no longer growl.

When I was a child,
I'd tip him slightly backwards
to make him audible,
the sound from a box-like thing
embedded in his chest.

The noise he made
wasn't anything *close*
to a bear's,
wouldn't frighten a *fox*
at all,
his voice more like
some rubbery monster
from a vintage Toho flick.

The bear in my closet
is sitting on a shelf,
behind a hanging black shirt
and some poetry books
that I've never bothered to read.

I haven't worn the shirt in years.
It's chafed around the collar,
gone stiff along the cuffs.

There's nothing in that closet
worth keeping,
its main occupant
quiet
like some death row inmate
praying silently with a priest,

dreading the *rustle*
of a plastic green bag
as if it's an electric chair.

## My Cat is Half-Greek,
## or Zeus left the Acropolis open again

My cat communes
with the mythical, with the infinite
and glorious invisible,
getting an inside track
on the weather
and when the sky's
about to change its tune.

My cat tells me
when it's going to rain outside,
by the way she wiggles her whiskers
and tilts her head
beside the bathroom wall.

My cat knows instinctively
when it's going to pour
in Noachian proportions,
when the neighbours
will pound the door
and beseech us to let them in,
their basements flooded
and the water still rising.

Silly cat, tumbling around
with slanted head
and twitching whiskers.
I'm only turning on the shower.
Go back to your bed of sleep –
and *dream*
of chasing moths
in the garden,
the sun brighter
than an Orion Nova
and your shadow in pursuit
as you run.

Let's not talk of storms today
despite the warnings
you sense from above:

Perhaps those sounds you hear
are the thunderous applause
from the pantheons up from their seats,
as Taurus snags the matador,

the rumbling
that of Hercules in hunger,
starving for the love of Deianeira,
she who causes his eyes
to overflow
with spit and drizzle,
a few simple sobs
to remind us men and beasts
that the deities too
feel that which pains us all,
blotting out the sun
when there's none to share
their sorrow.

Or it may only be Aphrodite
calling you in for your dinner,
unaware you have a home
with *me*,
cavorting with the mortals
because we bow to your meows
and your purrs,
our closest, intimate link
to both the eternal
and the divine.

**The excuse I use
to avoid cleaning under the stairs**

How lonely it must be
to be a spider
in the basement,
one that's sitting on its web,
in a corner without light,
awaiting that *rare* arrival,
the hoped-for,
off chance encounter,
when an insect-thing
will venture where it knows
it really shouldn't,
get trapped in sticky white,
kick its hair-like limbs
in a panic,
sensing deep-down in resistance
that the end has inevitably come,
there's no escaping this alive,
feeling the webbing
beginning to bounce
as its maker at last approaches.

I sometimes have to wonder
if the spider ever pities,
considers *mercy* for a moment,
seeing its tiring victim struggle
in the seconds before the kill,
being tempted,
not by pangs
of some *compassion,*
but by those of *isolation,*
supplanting that of hunger
and its drive to feed and hunt;

taking an instant to say *hello,*
in its own spidery way,

enjoy the twinning breath
of *company,*
a meeting of insect/arachnid eyes,
wish it could *share* a tale or two,
get to know this flying creature,
fellow cellar-dweller, *better,*

hope there's no karma-bearing grudge
or vengeance *doled* by divinity,
that its prey will understand,
know the slaying isn't personal,
that the pinch and bite are quick,
that the blood that's drained
is a *gift,*
gratefully received,

that *calming* sleep comes first,
so deep in life's last ebbing
there'll be the precious chance
to dream.

**His and Hers**

In clashing closets,
your reds mimic my blacks
in starch and wrinkles,
in pleats unkempt
and the way that mothballs
keep our earwigs at bay.

When we were younger,
we shared our cramped enclosures,
complemented pinks with blues,
folded every sock
and cashmere sweater,
high heels and tennis shoes
conjoined in copulation.

Now they're flung across the bedroom
after a brutal day at work
or an aggressive walk
from the bus stop,

butts of cigarettes
scenting the soles,
broken snaps and laces
securing our silence.

**Fish Out of Water**

It's no one else's business, really,
why Martha did what she did,
or why she made the mistake
of stepping outside the bounds
where geeks with glasses
should never dare to tread.

Perhaps she got tired of sharing lunch
with the Chess Club,
or wolfing down her sandwich
amidst a hurried rush to the library
lest some thought her friendless
if she stayed in the cafeteria
to eat alone.

An " L" on the forehead
may only come off with gasoline,
but why torch the whole house
and take your parents with you?
Why not leave them
to find you in a state of grace,
yielding to the punishment
that served them best?

Why not drop a handmade pompom
at your feet,
letting them recall the day
the homeliest girl in school
tried out for cheerleading,
so they may indeed know
at least *one* reason
why they saw you swinging
from the end of a ragged noose,
your diary turned to a blank page
where your first kiss should have been?

**Just Friends**

In this, your final visit,
we talk of "only friends"
and the other silly things
that make us look away,
from each other's eyes,
when neither you or I
would want it this way.

And I change the subject
rather hastily,
when you ask
*am I still pretty?*
Its catch twenty-two
stares me in the face
when I speak in lieu
of suitcase bombs
and bio wars
that make for front page fodder.

*I don't want to die unloved*
you say and I agree,
and a gas bar clerk
is shot five times
as if once
won't do the trick,
bread lines grow in Montreal
and the Budget calls for higher tax
that moms can never give;

and Jihad's called again,
stocks are set to crash,
and I think you're just as pretty
as the day we danced to Liszt,

and I speak of strikes instead,
of whales harpooned
and seals still killed for fur,

of famines in Angola
and that nukes are everywhere,

and I'd like to kiss you now
but I'm too afraid to try
and land mines blow
six kids apart
and ain't it great
to be alive.

**Maybe**

When you turned to me
and raised your brow,
I too made a face.
He sauntered past:
straggly, dishevelled,
fourth-hand clothes
still rank with beer and soot.

The little girl beside him
was clean and bright
and smelled of soap.
Maybe he was her father
or her granddad.
Maybe a stranger she befriended
as he panhandled,
in front of the candy store
a block away.
Maybe he had a few pennies to spare
and bought her gumballs
instead of the cigarettes
we assumed he craved.

Maybe he was gentle-hearted
and didn't fondle her at night
when owls made their perch
and roosters knew their time
was coming.

**Seven Day Rental**

One of my students borrowed
*La Maison du Plus Pied*
by Jean-Pierre D'Allard,
telling the rise, fall
of the Sainte Bouviers,
ensnared by riches,
hatreds spawned
and business won, lost,
won & lost.

She recounts her favourite scene
towards the end,
where a liberated Marie
slaps the face
of her brutal husband, Serge,
played by an aging
Stephane DeJohnette.

It's the one-eighty,
the turning point for both characters,
the moment where love
drops its transcendence,
its fixed and static state.

I think Anise, my student,
sporting occasional welts
that I ask nothing about,
has found a muse
to lift her trampled spirit
as she says
"the film, the film."

Yes it is such.

**November Rose**

It's a Jane or Johnny-come-lately,
the solitary rose in my garden,
a harvest holdover or belated bloom
that's risen when the others have died.

It has none to compete for attention,
isn't lost in a sea of red.

I ponder its predicament,
think of it as lonely,
regretting it hadn't blossomed sooner
when the buzz of flying insects
were droning their affection.

I'll water it in the evening,
as stars speck the sky in Autumn's cool.
I'll sing it to sleep
as I retire,
pray for grace
should the frost strike swift.

**Moss**

There are crops of spongy green
creeping steadily over stones,
scaling *up* the trunks of trees,
the ones both living and fallen,
and there are dabs of deep moss
filling vacancies in earth,
their scents filling lungs
in this autumn/sunshine stroll.

Look at how little needs to be done:
they don't ask us to water their roots,
mow their tops or manicure,
yet theirs is a shade so grand
that even the wealthiest lawns
in the land
are only stubble,
pale in their blades of envy.

**For Mr. Bannister, who delivers flowers to most of the people on my block**

If anyone's worth the pity,
it's the delivery guy I know,
the man who works for the florist –
must be close to 65 by now.

He lost his darling mum
when he was just a little boy,
works 16 hours on Mother's Day,
spreading bears and bright bouquets
to all the matriarchs and much-loved.

I wonder how it must wound
and rip his beating insides open,
driving dozens of pink/red roses around
on bloody St. Valentine's Day,
a lonely gentleman as he
who's never married
or been engaged.

I picture his coming home
to some dilapidated apartment
in the city's shitty end,
where the junkies and the lost
spend the rest of their miserable nights,

imagining he brings them leftovers
from the azaleas unaccepted,
from the carnations cast aside,
saying they have a secret admirer,

or leaving them instead
in a bout of indulgence
beside the crack of his own front door,
pretending there's a woman out there
who truly loves him enough
to send him only the very best.

## Penny & The Englishman

Look right up the stairs
and you'll see her,
with her tired, spectacled eyes
and flowing hair
of greying brown.

All that doesn't matter,
you tell me.
She's still as pretty as sin
and stands in line
at all the busy transit stops,
hoping one's his get-off point
but it never seems to be.

She's bled her life away
you whisper
as if it's a game,
a starling's secret,
misadventure
played to the nines
and tarnished dreams
made bright
by a single jiffy wipe.

One fine day
she'll spot him
in a flash,
pick him out
from the morning throng,
and then we'll pause
for overtime,
to see if the wait
was worthy
and if skin that's pruned
tastes sweet.

**On the Difference a Single Minute Can Make**

I'm finding myself
forever late
and running a frantic catch-up
to every place
I need to be:

The bus booting off
as I stretch my waving arms
to flag it down;

The opening credits rolling
as I scramble for my seat,
popcorn spilling
from its bag;

Missing the girl I would have met –
*and married* –
had I seen her seconds sooner,
*before* a line of people
blocked our path,
leaving us as strangers,
our eyes to never lock.

I lost out
on a stellar career
because I didn't see the want ad
in the paper –
the listing stamped for me
under the arm
of another seeker,
who snagged the final copy
of the city's daily news
just a breath-and-a-half before.

I want to ask my mother
why she couldn't birth me faster,

why she hadn't heeded
the contractions
just as soon as they were felt,
without delay,

pushed an extra bit harder
when my head was popping out,

that additional minute of life,
that little head start,
giving me adequate time to stroll
to that bus stop down the street,
smell some flowers along the way,
tell a girl I think she's lovely,

if we can meet for a funny movie
when my day at the office is done.

**For every poet who knows what it's like**

There's a woman in the front row
who has started to cough.

I've spent seven hours
on a stinky bus
to get here,
to read poetry in this bookshop,
in front of fifty-six people
and now one of them
is coughing up a squall,
doing a fabulous seal simulation,
lacking only flippers and an inflatable ball.

The store had laid out padded chairs
and a table full of books –
my latest and those
of a trio of poets
who'd read before my turn had come:

in feather-dropping silence,
in monastic quietude,
in that attentive hush that happens
when the audience is rapt in words.

I raise my voice in hopes of drowning
the woman's incessant hacks,
bellowing *there's truth in affirmation
and in eyes that see past stars!*

And my pacing is off,
my inflection is chaotic,
my ability to focus
easily thwarted
by her gurgling phlegm.

I want to stop abruptly –
ask her
what her problem is,
if she's a smoker who's never quit,
if she waited for *me* to begin my set
before unleashing her pent-up noise.

But I forge on in a smouldering stride,
thankful I've saved
my favourite poem
for the climactic denouement,
*grateful* she's just left her seat
and gone off to the back of the shop,

where, if I'd been more attentive,
I would have noticed the coffee bar,
the gleam
of frothing machines,
figured she might forego
the Buckley's,

embrace the whirr
that cappuccinos bring.

**William of Carlton Press**

I've heard you hoard
your favourite drink
when you're depressed,
sigh to the light
of a single lamp,
sip Beaujolais
and play
Clark Terry 45's,

the jazzman
who never got the lauds
of Miles Davis,
nor was spun as much
as 'Trane,

your eyes scanning pages
of Seamus Heaney
and beloved Bowering,
our poet laureate
and honoured fellow,

your veins draining wine
from your head,
*red red wine*, you sing alone
in a cappella,

never making shortlists
or signing Griffin's winner,

learning that highs,
not lows,
come by writing
something grand,
with choice imprint,

not by bleeding
out your chequebook,
filling basements
with your boxes,

mistaking bookstore whispers
for your name.

**Bullets**

I want to toast
and commend you
on your debut publication,
in that journal of arts and letters,
the one from Warsaw, in English,
though there's a bit of perplexing Polish
sprinkled about,
basil for the borscht, so to speak.

And in it you wail as a Banshee,
about that Irish brother of yours,
signing up for Bush and Blair
and all the blood that smells
of petrol.

Like him, you set yourself alight
with your poem on random bullets,
their anonymity,
how most of them
miss their mark,
lie flat in their innocence,
or wedged in the greater distance
where the sidewalk meets the street,
between blocks on boulevards,
in bricks of banks
and buildings,

that only one
in forty-seven
pierces bone, fragments flesh,
is cursed by sons and daughters
and the woman who becomes a widow
the very moment that she is told,

asked if she'll identify,
verify,

keep the flag
that drapes the coffin,
possess a plaque
that bears a face.

**They Asked Me to Write a Poem Against the War but I Only Came Up With This**

It's not about borders
or bombs at all,
or guerillas in camouflage
or secret air raids in the night,
when presidents are sleeping
and the warlords
are dancing two-steps
till the dawn.

It isn't about the prisoners
encamped by fences
or the tanks
carving tracks
in Arab sand,
or the manner in which
white leaflets drop
warning masses
of impending doom.

It doesn't mean a thing
that missiles rotate
in secret silos
underground,
or warheads
crown their apex
with coordinates
set in place.

It's about the brother
you called a fag,
the girl across the street
you said was gross,

the kid rebuffed
on corners
'cause he's black
and sporting "Pistons"
on his shirt,

that suburban shoppers
are quick to make assumptions –

about the businessman
you assume
cares for nothing
other than cash,
the twins you feel are the same
and soldiered commies
if shy Chinese,
the hatred seeded
in budding hearts
when you murmur *children
keep your distance.*

## Just another coup d'état

When he opened the account
we called him *Jonas,*
cheques and balances
as gold cuff links
without a scratch.

The business thrived,
he hired and fired
without conscience or remorse
and the ties that bind
were locked
in stocks and bonds.

We gasped and called him *Daniel*
when he gave it all away,
save the dollar that he placed
in a child's outstretched hand,
saying *invest as seeds*
*in those who thirst*
*and hunger,*
*one fine day*
*they'll bless you*
*with a poem*
*expressed as thanks,*
*moving you to toss aside*
*the finest pearls*
*for nuts that squirrels*
*can treasure.*

It made no sense:
the words, the deeds,
why he lives in cold damp hostels
and gives his kisses to the poor.

Perhaps he saw a vision
of his death
amid the mansions
and the yachts,
the loneliness
of beach front homes
when there's no one to see
the sunset with.

Or maybe Wall Street lions
took the life of someone dear
and he takes a second chance
to get it right, to make amends,
to pet the heads of puppies
he once shook his gilded
briefcase at.

## Orange Hall, 585

You're scolding me again,
for wisecracks
that aren't funny,
for my pointing out
that the "Orange Hall"
across the road
*isn't* orange
but a dirty beige and brown.

*Why don't they call it*
*'The Beige*
*and Brown Hall'?*
I utter in jest –
and I chuckle alone,
as I always seem to do.

The truth of the matter is
I can't recall
who the Orangemen are,
if they're Protestant
or if they wear those silly hats
like the Shriners
or Buffaloes.

*I bet they like oranges*
I quip a second time,
and your rolling eyes
are a sullen response,
set in action
by a wretched pun
or two,

or the thought
of a Catholic friend,
caught in the crossfire
of a Belfast parade,
when you were young
and laughed at jokes
so miserably long ago.

## Unborn Daughter, or Why I live with Cats

I fear for you and what's ahead:

Wars of race and hatred,
cities bombed and shelled,
skeletons of bone and stone
and fresh water dried to sand,
radiation in the land
and even if there's not,
if it doesn't come to pass,
how can I let you
out of doors
with the bad man there
and waiting?

**Trumpet Player**

Trumpet player,
tell me you fight the backward mind
of *the man* and his corps
of soldiers, stomping off
to office towers, elevators,
cubicles and charts,
graphs and bars,
pills and bars.

Do your solo and your thing,
the squall of sound
that lets me know the anger
of your race
and the *family* left behind
in run-down walk-ups
strewn with bottles,
cigarettes.

Sweat from your brow
under hot blue light
and rail against its calm,
tip the scales both low and high
and do it poetically.

Trumpet player,
play for *her,*
the one you loved, now gone.
Make it seem
that flags have dropped
with sailors dead at sea.

**This is all you learned
from your trip to the tabloid stand**


That walking isn't as pleasant
as you'd envisioned,
your memories
like the brazen cars
behind you,
*running* amber lights
and spitting smoke,
indifferent on
your quest to cross the street,
the man who's selling news
annoyed by pennies
you say you're short.

That the Prince of Wales
will be Charles the Third
and King for twenty days,
expiring from wear and age,
just weeks after
his "Methuselah" mum,
waiting for Godot and for what?

That your sneakers
are tearing suddenly
in the rain,
that they are cheap,
that leaves clog the sewers
and your socks are soaking wet,
to microwave
a dumb idea,
thinking they'll warm and dry,
not guessing
they'll start to flame,
the firemen
becoming angry
when they see the reason why.

That *in* a crowded hospital,
your mother's stuck in bed,
on the 10th
or 11th floor,
you really can't remember
because you never *visit* her,
save the time you needed money,
brought her crosswords
but in *Dutch,*
discarded in the dumpster
behind the Starbucks' coffee shop,
and you never bothered to check
if they were *English*
or ever solved.

That somewhere on the beach
in Monaco,
celebrities plunge in surf,
*bake* in Mediterranean sun,
hope they're properly buffed
and waxed
lest paparazzi
snap their flaws.

That you'd wanted
to breathe some blooms
throughout this morning's
mile walk,
foregoing the check
on forecasts,
too impatient to read
at home,
the soggy pages ripping
as they're turned,
the wind smelling more
and more of worms.

## Chelsea and Liverpool

I asked you
where you were going
and you replied
*I need to be out in the world*
*to write about the world*
and I thought to follow you
but checked myself in time.

I've no right to pry
and spy at what you see –
bring a coloured binder with you
and jot down what you feel –

I'll be at home, on the couch,
watching English Football
and eating pickles from the jar.

And we'll hear it *all* –
the curses, the cheers,
the upheaval of the crowds
and their disenchantment,
and you'll nail the winning header
just before the final whistle,
the man shooting heroin
on the sidewalk
that brings forth a gasp,
the punctured veins
that keep things
from being forgotten,
tied at nil.

## At the Tone: 17 hours, 46 minutes, Coordinated Universal Time

It all occurred in the course
of a rooftop pigeon's blink:

the homeless streaming
into lofty bank towers
decreed low-cost housing
by politicians who truly gave a damn,
bankers themselves
saying to hell with the profits
and building wells and clinics
in the horn of Africa,
Africans feeding their own
with manna that snows
from the hands of a loving God
who really *does* exist,
killing in his name ceasing
with the "clang!" of a million bayonets
being thrown to the ground
at the same splinter of being,

and on a darkened street in Copenhagen,
a skinhead hugs a Jew
he would have beat with a club
only seconds before,
Hell's Angels pop wheelies
as they bring canned goods
to a hospice for ex-hookers,
Colombian cartels burn their hash & heroin,
Jerry Springer talks quantum physics on the BBC,
while in a gnarled thicket
in the woods of Minnesota,
Ted Nugent drops a shotgun
at the foot of a deer
he embraces as a son,
which on second thought
*needn't* fall and bleed
when all is said and done.

**12/01/07**

In this warmer-than-normal winter,
the trees are budding early,
in mid-January's
rain-instead-of-snow.

I feel I ought to go outside
and *bring* some soothing tea,
*play* a tranquil song
for harp and strings,
softly tell a bedtime story,

be the sandman for a spell,
*send* the rousing leaves-to-be
*back* into their shells,

lest the winds return from the north,
puddles freeze over, and greening branches
waken to a bird-less lie of ice.

## Decaf to go

I thought she watched me as I wrote,
a girl with beret cliché,
Irish cream and lemon Danish,
who'd smoke a cigarette if legal
but it's not;

and she's reading Schulz and Robert Frost
and the many roads to heaven
and I thought to ask her what she thought
of love and death and living
amid our own sel-
fish carte blanche.

She wasn't there, really,
nor am I – we weave and thread
and move about
as atoms from the sun,
that settled here so predisposed
to birth and fear and loathing.

I see her sometimes, singing praise
when the *moon* is halved
and the evening tide
pulls *cold,*
when the waitress looks
for dollar tips
and the closing chimes
ring sweet,

and I have no time to end the verse
with lights that cue to leave,
the sax that fades to hush,
and the cop who walks the beat
looking through the tinted window,
hat tipped in hello,
ideally dreaming of a night
without a single shout
or crime.

**Queens & Richmond**

You said his name was Maynard
and he squeegees for a dime.

*Fine then.* I dig for better
coinage, much to my
chagrin. *A toonie
for the back
and leave the mirrors
filled with spots.*

When you catch my face
from behind the car,
I'll have excuse
for imperfection.

## The Artists' Long Weekend

It was supposed to be
a day off from the squabbles,
from the debates on right & wrong
and the five stone pillars
of Western Imperialism.

Saturday I like you best.
You leave your texts behind
and Naomi Woolfe is kept
in white sheep's cloth,
talk of apple cobblers, chocolate sprinkles,
as deep in thought as we'll ever get
but not today:

You battle greedy parking meters,
wage war on 10 cent hikes,
relive the Russian Revolution
and complain of cookies
looking better than they taste.

*Let us leave the bakery,*
I say in reckless suggest,
offering to whisk you
to splendoured heights
and the flashing bulbs of theatre.

You counterpunch,
and the Museum it is,
old relics left to rust
behind coloured Chinese glass,
and sculptures chipped & shorn.

*We're the only ones here,*
we slump and sigh, with nothing more to see,
our disappointment
bouncing off the walls
as van Gogh in a straitjacket
would have.

## Bitter Jeez Louise

The raincoat that she dons,
on sunny days, makes them laugh:
the girls in tank and halter tops,
the boys on black skateboards,
even grandmas walking dogs.

She spends her spring
in stack 9B,
section E point six-four-three.
She's working on a thesis,
I've heard,
from the driver on my route:
how fossil fuels
can be replaced
by solar panels,
westward winds.

"Louise" never smiles
when she boards the city bus,
her change dropped like anchors
from her hands.

*She gave her quarters*
*all to bullies, learned to study*
*without lunch.*

Even now,
she sits in corner cubicles,
eyes graffiti scrawled of her,
twelve years past,
has yet to scratch it out
or eat a sandwich,
soup, at noon.

**The Substitute**

The receptionist mentions "Dr. Devon"
and I flashback for half a moment.

*Devon* was the kid in twelfth grade,
overdosed at a party,
had just been dumped
by his girlfriend, Lindy,
who was there,
with her linebacker-boyfriend,
and the 40 or so
who crowded around
his crumpled, breathless figure
found in the moldy,
clammy basement.

Dr. Devon is filling in today
for Dr. Taberwicz,
taking temperatures,
hearing heart-rates,
prescribing pills
for the sick,
soon-to-be-dying.

## She's the Bookworm of Santo Domingo

William Faulkner's got his hold on you
with Gretna Green and Ernestine
but he's really not the bard
you thought he was
because he hasn't made you cry
like Cohen does when he's on his game
or Emily because you knew she lived alone
in that big old house
when she should have been on her back
and getting laid.
Such passion.

Sylvia Plath married an ingrate
who became the laureate,
the toast of the town
but you know that rascal Ted
lost out in the end
and she was quite the swimsuit charmer –
and a poet to boot.

Your softest spot's for Henry Miller
and his *Rosy Crucifixion,*
and though your mother thinks it's literary,
you know it's just a cunning way
to do the porno *without* the getting caught.

But Nabokov's your idol
because he told it like it is
and every middle-aged teacher
you've ever known
has yearned to fondle your budding breasts
and painting toenails is just the appetizer
for something deeper.

*Leaves of Grass* is Whitman's triumph
and makes you look respectable
when you carry it around,
a discman strapped around your waist,
Gregorian chants filling your ears
when you should have been listening
to the boy running behind you,
heart a thunder,
staining his pants and calling your name.

## Alexander Schmidt

The rumours started
in 5th grade gym:
he never changed in public,
was last when picked on teams.

*He was the ugliest kid on the block.*

Do the math and fund a study:
children flock to beauty,
assign our sins to those without.

*The pet store girls, all tanned and twee,*
*shrunk back from awkward glances.*

I didn't know all this,
that symmetry is front and centre,
that his eyes were blue and brown.

*Was he handsome in his dreams,*
*in his French class reveries?*

You say he went home sick –
on 2/14,
with nothing on his desk,
while even the custodian
was seen
with paper hearts
that peeked from pockets.

*We felt much better, about ourselves,*
*when crushing him like salt.*

He skulked about so creepily
and sat near monkey bars.
He liked to sing to nimble kids
with his messy, uncut hair.

*They blared out "leper"
with five bull horns,
the barber changed his look.*

He was fired, pumping gas,
lived on Welfare, Luke & John.
He painted pictures for a smoke,
buskered for a smile.

*He liked the winter, he did.
Ski-masks made him human.*

## On Our Search for Leonard Cohen
## and Maybe One of His Many Lovers

> *If I am dumb beside your body*
> *while silence blossoms like tumors on our lips*
> *it is because I hear a man climb stairs*
> *and clear his throat outside our door*
>
> Leonard Cohen, from "Poem"
> in *Let Us Compare Mythologies*

The expenditure is worth it
you contend,
hundreds for a train
that stank of fish,
a hotel with no TV,
the cost of wine and dining
and the tip we never left,
lapping lukewarm lattes
under awnings of cafés.

Yes, I too have heard the stories
of his coming,
every so often,
to his haunts in Montréal,
the *bridge* that spans the river
though we argue on which one,

the kiosk in the market
where *Suzanne* was given birth,
amid the lemons
and yellow beans,
the singer seeing the sun
in all those tints
and tones of fruit,
how its setting were tangerines,
the moon a whitish melon
giving muse.

I dispute your speculation,
say the woman
the tune was named for
didn't cook or squeeze
a lime,
that you've confused her
with someone else,
an unnamed mistress
from a stanza
of his *Poem*.

We can always
look for *her,*
her features gone to prune,
dentures getting stuck
on autumn apples,

purple veins
about her calves
and swollen feet
that scrape the ground
around her cane,

never
measuring up
to *Marianne,*
her existence
only words
without a song.

## Franklin Stein

It was all a matter of perspective
to their Uncle Franklin,
an odd creature of sorts they said,
not only because he put two spoons of coffee
in a cup of sugar,
or held a ball of melting ice cream
in his hand –
eating the tip of a wafer-cone;

but that he was a man who showered
before he jogged,
who once bought a car
with rolls of pennies, thirty-thousand of them,
and used a crisp, Victorian-hundred
to get a gumball he quickly finished
after the sixth or seventh chew.

His niece and nephew were aghast
when they brought him to church
and he stood in front of the righteous,
making the sign of the cross
and forgiving them their sins:
*In the Name of the Mother,*
*the Daughter,*
*and Casper the Friendly Ghost.*

His Doctor was amazed
that he made it past 40:
eating the peels of oranges,
of bananas, green & yellow,
discarding the fruit of both –
picking the grapes off
to devour the stems,
spitting out cherries
to swallow the pits.

He pulled out the grass
so the weeds might thrive,
fed the mice & roaches
only the finest cheese and caviar,
and married the fattest girl in town
after *breaking* a model's heart,
saying beauty was in the eye
of the beholder.

## Vodka Bill

Takes to the bottle
as soon as he's through the door.

But this isn't one of those miserable
alcoholic poems.
Bill can hold his liquor,
is rarely reeling drunk
and his liver functions fine.
He has no wife or kids to beat
but would never do that anyway.

You see, it's just something he does,
one-third vodka, two-thirds
orange juice and Coke.
Forget his vows to move away
and find someone who loves him,
move away
to that grander job
eluding him to this day.

There's nothing wrong
with Wal-mart blue,
with spending his nights alone,
practicing "hello" and "how are you?"
and "can I help you find anything?"
and maybe he simply likes the taste
and wouldn't have it
any other way
and it's not so bad for
"do you love me?"
to go unanswered
in his dreams
and in the shoe department,
runners to the right,
slippers to the left.

## The Violinist

I'll wait for you in the foyer,
alit by a chandelier
and streetlamps seen from the window sill.

I'll be sitting in the velvet chair,
an antique too good to touch
but hardwood floors should not be soiled
by shoes I've muddied in the rain.

As I dry, your lesson will come to a close,
and the student you're in love with
will leave some angel cake as thanks,
for teaching her Dvořák,
his cycle of *Cypress Trees*,
perhaps unbeknownst of its origins,
how Antonín was inspired to write it,
loving Josefina, his pupil in Prague,
watching her marry another
and leave him a muse to scribe his work.

You will keep her gift in the freezer,
not daring to warm in an oven, eat
and be left with only the crumbs.
You'll buy tickets for two to the Symphony,
the Number 6, in D Major,
with me as your reluctant guest;

and from a concealing balcony
you'll boast of your protégé,
that she's a violist
and cellist as well.
You'll say the pastoral sequence forthcoming
is her finest musical moment,
her strings ascending the others
in an overture to *you,*
and it's only an ill-timed sneeze
from the audience
that keeps me from hearing it as so.

## On Our Meeting in the Lunchtime Rush

Of course, your hair had changed,
pinned-up, either for a new, mature look
or because of some dress code
you had to follow,
for this deli counter in the marketplace,
the one I haven't been to in a while
and it's quite apparent I hadn't
or else I never would have stopped
to grab a stupid club-on-rye.

Two things seemed to shock you:
my ordering of animal flesh
I'd disavowed several years before
(though I could have convincingly said
it was for my carnivorous colleague at work)
and the scruffy beard I'd grown,
tie loosened below the neck,
much more grey than you'd expect
after a meagre, single year.

But keep in mind, my ex,
I had higher expectations of *you:*
a business degree,
Marketing 101,
not this "Four ninety-five please" rubbish
that takes me aback,
your delivery colder than ham
from the ice box, your demeanour sour
as mayo left out for hours,
neglected, flies encircling,
with your failure to acknowledge my name,
how I'd been, if I'd been dating again.

There was a moment, though,
my former paramour,
when our brown eyes *locked* instead of blinked,
a millisecond of understanding,

you sensing I'd never meant those words
I screamed so many months ago,
my reading of your "Thank you, have a nice day"
as a fraying string of hope
that I might soon, again,
visit this counter, this *Fritz's Delicatessen,*
order the vegetarian special,
jasmine tea,
pretend we've both re-found our love
or at least *simulate* that we're civil,
anything, anything other than this.

**The Devotion**

Without your daily nags
I can't imagine what I would do:

Your ridiculing of my neckties
that are Pisa-like
in their slants,
how my hair and beard
need trimming,
and how I'm glued
to Sports-TV.

Vex me further,
oh one who decries my faults:
tell me how the towels
are soiled and squished
on the bathroom hooks;
bellow how lazy
I surely am
to leave our dog
without its morning walk;

that the grass is a jungle
and why don't I cut it?
Or finally fix
the backyard swing
that wobbles
though it's never in use?

And if I patch the hole
in the driveway,
water the chestnut tree
that sags,
will you mix my favourite drink,
promise sex
that says I'm beloved?

## One Nine-Hundred

The couple in the porno ad
are not in love,
and you're likely right
though I said there's
a chance.

*There's always a chance,*
you replied.
I think about *always*
and glance at your wisp
of auburn hair,
looking away before you
catch me.

**Listening**

I shouldn't be eavesdropping
on the young women next to me,
at this café, as I feign
the reading of a book
and the listening
to piped-in jazz.

I shouldn't have a clue
that the blonde is having trouble
with her boyfriend,
that he's a dolt, inconsiderate,
that he gave her nothing special
for Christmas,
aside from broken chocolates,
re-gifted from a day before,
from a relative that he hates
and she knows he didn't buy them,
that she put so much thought
into *his* present
which he barely acknowledged

and then her friend one-ups her,
lamenting the bruises on her arm
that she reveals with the tug of her sleeve,
and amid the cut-off gasp, Billie Holiday's
*Mean to me* kicks in,
which I'll nervously tap my fingers to,
pretending I haven't heard a thing.

## The haiku I just wrote is pointless

What's the point of

*Layers of grey cloud
are leaving the landscape wet
Ducklings in the grass*

a critic asked me,
saying who cares about ducks
in the grass and why would anyone
read a poem about them
and I emphasized duck*lings*
which are the babies
and people are always drawn to babies
because they're cute and in this case
they're fuzzy and walk in a row
after their mother
and the mother isn't mentioned in the haiku
if you'll notice
and the point might be that they're lost,
maybe orphaned,
that the grey cloud leaving the landscape
was far more vicious than we realize,
casting mother duck away in a storm
and her babies doing an awkward waddle
in search of her and tell me then
that you don't even care

## Tokyo

In Tokyo, it is tomorrow.

As I go about today, noting
each error that I've made,
all the snap and hasty decisions
that haven't worked
as I had planned,
I think how the Japanese
are waking *up* to a warming sun
and that they're not entirely
on their own:

Australians, Filipinos,
Koreans and Chinese;
Vietnamese, Indonesians
and some far-east Russians too,

all getting a jump on existence,
18 hours or so ahead
(compared to *Canadian* me, that is),
knowing the markets in advance,
the trends, what will be popular this day,
how to escape the pitfalls that awaited
yesterday;

kissing a loved one while at lunch
as I *dive* in the dreams of night.

They'll be roughly three-quarters
of a rotation
smarter than me,
having learned from the foolish mistakes
I've yet to make, able to guide me,
if they could, from afar.

I want to hop on a streaking jet
and race across the globe,
just beyond the speed of sound,
land at Narita International,
dine on sushi and yakisoba,
discover what living should be about.

And before the moon
makes a glowing swath
*across* the star-filled sphere,
I'll hurry home,
to the familiarity
of Eastern Time,
re-living the calendar moment
though from another point on the Earth:

remembering
to hold the elevator
for the blind man
and his dog,
answer the cell call from my boss
without a snarl
or flippancy,
avoid the racing
of yellow lights
and the *cursing*
of pedestrians,

let my wife know
that I love her
instead of complaining
of rice that sticks.

**Pacifica**
            *– for T.*

I've taken the liberty
of casting my lines
across the sand,
without symmetry,
to be smudged underfoot by toddlers
stomping their heels
along the shore.

It's heresy, I know,
this verse I scribe in your honour,
this floundering way of writing,
this unschooled manner of
spitting out words like *siren,
enrapture, infinity,*
that may mean nothing to you at all

and that a starfish snags on rock
at lowest tide
is irrelevant to both of us
but I make note of it anyway,
in case I need a reason
to speak on matters bleak
but beautiful,
in lieu of love
and poems.

the author

Andreas Gripp has written seven books of poetry
and is involved in community radio in
London, Ontario, where he lives with his cats,
"Clea" and "Sheba". He also writes fiction and
essays and hopes to plant a successful
vegetable garden someday.

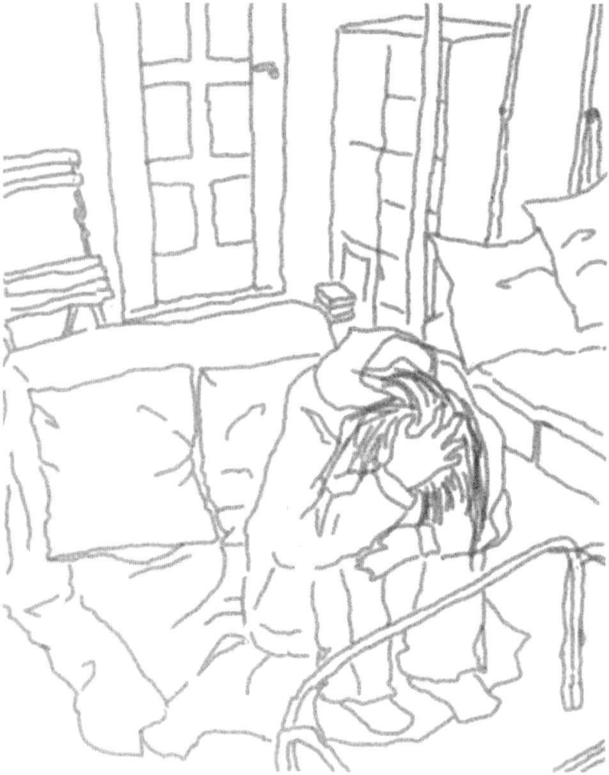